Fo

Four Corners of Grace

Four Corners of Grace

Four Corners of Grace

Suicide takes one life and traumatizes many others. The chaos, unanswerable questions, and unimaginable pain create a feeling of stumbling through utter darkness. So where can a person turn when a loved one takes his or her own life? Let David Staal take you on a valuable, yet vulnerable journey toward hope found in Four Corners of Grace.

Peter Newhouse, PhD, LMSW, ACSW
CEO of Winning At Home, Child and Family Wellness Center

As a former pastor who has dealt with the devastating impact of suicide in families and congregations, I would have been grateful for the opportunity to offer Four Corners of Grace as a resource to bereaved families and friends. Author David Staal covers an amazing amount of ground in a remarkably brief volume as he describes how the simple act of extending grace can help heal the deepest wounds. Avoiding easy answers and simplistic platitudes, this book will be immensely helpful for all who wonder and weep over those who choose to end their own lives.

Reverend David Hughes, PhD
Retired Pastor of First Baptist Church Winston-Salem

I needed this.

Holly Payne
Mother of Tasha (May 31, 1975 – February 23, 2006)

Four Corners of Grace

Four Corners of Grace

when suicide takes someone you love

David Staal

Four Corners of Grace

Book interior design by Elise Sagmoe
Cover design by ENS Photography; ensphotography.net

ISBN (soft cover) 978-1-7343509-0-6
ISBN (e-format) 978-1-7343506-1-3

Scripture quotations marked (NLT) are taken from the Holy Bible, New Living Translation, copyright ©1996, 2004, 2015 by Tyndale House Foundation. Used by permission of Tyndale House Publishers, a Division of Tyndale House Ministries, Carol Stream, Illinois 60188. All rights reserved.

Scripture quotations taken from The Holy Bible, New International Version® NIV®
Copyright © 1973 1978 1984 2011 by Biblica, Inc. TM Used by permission. All rights reserved worldwide.

FourCornersofGrace.com

Four Corners of Grace

Four Corners of Grace

Four Corners of Grace

Teri
Memories will have to do,
but will never replace the real you.

Four Corners of Grace

Contents

Four Corners of Grace -Together- 1

Give-Myself-Grace Corner -Permission-................................9

Give-One-Another-Grace Corner -Purpose-.........................17

Give-God-Grace Corner -Comfort- 25

Give-Teri-Grace Corner -Freedom-......................................33

In Closing -Change-...41

Four Corners of Grace

Four Corners of Grace

-Together-

HOPE must have reasons. If no reasons exist, then it is just a dream. Maybe even a nightmare.

Today, the word "nightmare" may well describe your life. I know the feeling. The memory remains all too vivid of the moment my wife Becky received a 12:30 a.m. call to tell us that our lifelong friend Teri had taken her own life.

The words didn't seem real. Our involuntary glances bounced around the room, searching for something to make sense, and landed on nothing. Time slowed, which allowed the shock to fully tackle us. Every breath felt forced. Hard. Painful. Question after question arrived and, like uninvited guests, refused to leave. All this in the first 30 minutes. Two hours later we tried to fall asleep, hoping to wake up from this horrible dream.

But we couldn't. The suffocating feeling stayed with us, just as it probably has stayed with you. Life becomes overwhelming with enough pain. Especially right now—an abrupt, awful instance of eternity stealing someone from reality. Or, more bluntly, from you.

I want to help you breathe again without it hurting so much. To possibly fall asleep for a while tonight. Or maybe to just feel a moment of peace that loosens the knot in your stomach. The pages that follow won't try to solve anything, nor will they attempt to shortcut the grieving you need to do in order to fully heal.

We can, though, push aside a few of those torturous questions and clear an easier path for the next few days. Maybe longer. Along the way, we'll swerve well clear of trite religious sayings or—oh my—pontificated solutions to solving our society's suicide epidemic. Someone you love is gone; the circumstances are terrible; life hurts. And nothing else matters.

Wait, you and your pain matter. Let that truth sink in for a moment.

Every word you'll read exists to serve you. Most people will quickly sidestep the fallout from a suicide and, instead, fixate on the tragedy itself – how it happened, why it happened, or how to prevent it from happening again. Few, if any, will deliberately step into the proximity of the broken heart(s) left behind, because pain lathers up discomfort for all to feel. But the need to focus on yourself could not be more real. You've opened the right book. You're not alone.

It might seem counterintuitive or completely crazy, but this journey – unapologetically, yet compassionately -- walks toward and embraces the specific aches and anguishes suicide produces. Just like my wife and I had to do when Teri's family asked me to deliver the message at her funeral service. In the span of just a few short days, I had to rally from wanting to stay in bed all day to standing in front of a microphone. For reasons that will make sense a few pages from now, I felt like I owed Teri, so the only right answer to their request was yes.

Reading this book, though, requires only minimal commitment. Focus on just this moment and the single hour that follows. That's all. Make it through that sixty minutes and subsequent hours will become easier. Together, we will forge a way through very real, sometimes very raw words that will make sense only to those of us who, like you, have lost someone in such a cruel manner.

To start, imagine that you sat down a moment ago in the back pew at a crowded Tabernacle Church in Indianapolis, Indiana, on a cold February 6 afternoon. A man steps up to the microphone to deliver a message; his hands seem to tremble. That was me and yes, I felt scared. Specifically, I feared that ugly emotions would come spraying out, that I might fail to make it all the way to the end of the script, that my words would make no difference in such a large room filled with wounded hearts. But the emotions stayed in check, all the words were spoken, and they seemed to provide a much-needed perspective change for those who attended.

By the time we finish perhaps you, too, will discover that a small sliver of hope exists, accompanied by a reason to believe in it.

Whether you find hope or hope finds you, you'll have a chance to catch your breath.

To begin our journey, it may be helpful to consider ancient wisdom about facing such grief as we are experiencing. Although the Bible contains text written thousands of years ago, it holds words that articulate well what a broken heart might long to cry out in this very moment:

> *I will never forget this awful time, as I grieve over my loss.*
> *Yet I still dare to hope when I remember this:*

Four Corners of Grace

The faithful love of the Lord never ends!
His mercies never cease.
Lamentations 3:20-22 (NLT)

So let us come boldly to the throne of our gracious
God.
There we will receive his mercy, and we will find grace
to help us when we need it most.
Hebrews 4:16 (NLT)

A loved one's suicide turns normal life (if there is such a thing) into choppy and deeply uncomfortable space for everyone who must deal with the aftermath. This awful time is cruel and dark in ways the person who chose it as an escape could never imagine. But now, two paths exist for us: Give in to endless despair or go on a journey to find grace—right now, when we need it most.

The room you're in right now likely includes four distinct corners – and so does grace. We will briefly visit all four long enough to become familiar with the grace meant for you, for others, for God, and for the person you have lost. Steps worth taking, my friend, for good reason.

Suicide wants to believe it has had the last word. Don't allow such a thing! You now have the option to give one, two, three, or all four corners of grace the final say. In a situation you did not select and that no one deserves, this decision is now yours to make. How do you want this story to end?

Yes, finally you have a choice in all this—so let's visit the first corner.

Four Corners of Grace

Four Corners of Grace

Give-Myself-Grace Corner

-Permission-

PEOPLE prepare for many situations in life, but dealing with a suicide rarely receives forethought or pre-planning. Instead, folks must react.

Some crawl into deep introspective places within themselves, craving comfort from isolation. Others turn extremely active, hoping to outrun reality. A few will volley between the two extremes. While reactions vary, a curious common ground exists.

People often deal with the brutal reality that someone chose to end his or her own life by searching for answers in what seems like a landslide of mystery. We humans are an inquisitive bunch.

Suicide makes no sense, so applying energy to dig for every detail about the how, what, when, and where seems like the right thing to do. Such sleuthing can feel like a way to honor the person you lost, valiantly refusing to let him go. To not do so can feel like you don't care. And that's not true. After all, common sense might say, chasing down facts and discovering answers will eventually run its course and complete the seemingly unfinished story, right? Well, almost but not completely.

The real question – Why did she do it? – will forever remain just out of reach. A perfect position from which to torment you, by the way. But only if you let it. The choice is yours; chase after the mystery or choose a better way.

Welcome to the give-myself-grace corner.

For this corner to make sense requires a statement of tender truth that provides freedom you might not even realize you need: Nobody will ever know the full reason why our friend Teri made her decision, and no one likely will ever know why your loved one made the same fateful choice. Folks will speculate, but none will ever truly know why it happened.

Experts say that suicide is multicausal. For us, this means a complete understanding of all the variables will never happen. Two people can face the same life challenges and react in completely different ways. Although people might know the struggles a person faces, that list of problems will not add up to a logical conclusion to end life. Even when a note is left by the person, no one will read it and say, "This makes sense, so I can understand it all. Yes, this seems like it was the right thing to do."

The recipe that leads to suicide always contains a secret ingredient. For that reason, give yourself the grace – the permission – that it's okay to not figure out the full and final answer. Ever. No one will.

This truth defies our natural passion to discover reasons. When we find them, we can rest on those reasons. We can build upon them. We can trust them and, as a result, we can understand how life works. Except when life doesn't work.

The question Why? will remain unanswerable because only one person knows for sure. It's as if the reason is locked behind thick and sturdy doors, and your loved one (just like Teri) took the key with her when she left. The dark cloud of despair, confusion, and hopelessness that mysteriously blows into a person's life to convince her that suicide is the answer and now is the right time to do it, also slithers away without a trace. (That's the "secret ingredient" mentioned earlier.) Unless you can turn back time to join that moment and experience that cloud, your efforts to fully understand will fall short. Time only goes in one direction; the darkness is long gone and looking for the next person to pounce upon. Satisfied, no doubt, by the result—and the small seeds of doubt left behind that can quickly germinate into painful regret and self-incrimination.

The chronic absence of an answer to Why? creates space for me to wonder what role I played or could have played. Those of us left behind following a suicide should not blame ourselves, but often do anyway, through questions that serve only one purpose—to suggest guilt:

What if I had called?

What if I had said something different?

What if I had been more available?

Time spent trying to figure out what you could have done or said or noticed will push you into exhaustion, twist your brain in knots, and wreck your heart.

Hasn't enough damage been done? Yes it has, so take a different approach that will help your heart begin to heal.

When you choose to not solve the unsolvable or regret the hypothetical, then mental and emotional space will clear for you to fill with positive memories, words, and images. Do you miss her? Yes, of course. After all, you always miss those whom you truly love. Let grieving happen because the only way out of grief is to go through it. Along the way, though, grant yourself the permission to release the natural desire to unravel the big mystery.

Instead, take a deep breath and with all your might grab hold of something worth treasuring that will honor the person you lost.

Becky knew Teri from the time they were both born. Just days after Teri's suicide, Becky began to describe her friend with words that simultaneously embraced and defied the tragedy that had taken place: "Because Teri wasn't weighed down by having to manage a husband, she was free to love everyone around her. She was single but had the largest family of anyone I know."

The trade Becky made proved easy to see: Why obsess over Teri's tragic last moment when the opportunity exists to treasure a lasting memory? The former holds you captive; the latter sets you free. Lament the unanswerable or declare the undeniable. You choose.

Talk about your loved one by telling stories or sharing detailed descriptions of her to someone else. Or if you prefer, write words that only you'll read. List the funny aspects of her life, share how you met, your earliest memory, or what made her special. In whatever form has the most meaning for you, complete this sentence in as many ways as you can: I'll always remember how she...

Give yourself the grace to let that serve as a cherished memory to embrace and never let go.

In like manner, show yourself compassion if no smiles surface for a while, maybe longer. Tears, anger, and other emotions travel together in the grieving process, so welcome them all. They can peacefully coexist with the lasting memories you choose. As can laughter, when your time comes. A good friend who is a counselor has compassionately guided my walk (more like a crawl) through devastating times; now may be the right time for you to find a licensed, trained professional counselor who will do the same for you.

Once you're articulated what you prefer to remember, spend time in the give-myself-grace-corner and let the truth of these statements settle into your heart:

I don't know the reasons why and I will never know.

That doesn't mean I don't care or didn't love him.

I'm being honest with myself; it's okay that I don't know.

Nobody else knows why – and no one ever will.

I miss him and that's enough.

Say them to yourself. Over and over if needed. Write them in your own words. Share them with others. It took several repetitions over time for them to soak into my heart deep enough to become real.

Grace for yourself will help you deal with other people, our next chapter's focus. The decision to release the need to know why and, instead, to grab hold of the hidden blessings available from memories will prevent her death from stealing part of your life too.

Four Corners of Grace

"This day I call the heavens and the earth as witnesses against you that I have set before you life and death, blessings and curses.

Now choose life…"
Deuteronomy 30:19 (NIV)

Four Corners of Grace

Give-One-Another-Grace Corner

-Purpose-

SUICIDE forces a new reality upon the people it leaves behind. Unexpected. Uncomfortable. Inescapable. Whether in themselves or in others, no one knows how to navigate the awkwardness. No one knows how to deal with the pain. And no one knows what to say.

Welcome to the Give-One-Another-Grace Corner.

When Becky received the 12:30 a.m. call about Teri, she fell to the floor and wailed. Between sobs she choked out the words, "It's Teri. She's gone."

I joined her on the floor.

That surreal moment remains seared in my memory; the gravity of the news felt so heavy that we could only buckle under its weight. Becky and I have walked through life at its thickest before; her dad's death, my cancer battle, and more. But a suicide is different because it makes no sense. To me. To Becky. To you. To anyone. Keep hold of that truth—it will help you fully embrace the Give-One-Another-Grace Corner.

The word "grace" has a wide assortment of meanings, so let's establish a working definition for this as we continue our journey together through this book. To make it memorable, we'll use something simple and short: Unearned and unexpected love. This description will serve us well because the time has arrived to talk about other people, especially their need for grace from you and me.

They will need it, and you will benefit from sharing it with them.

Four Corners of Grace

In step with grace's two key components in our working definition, two types of people emerge. And oh yes, you'll recognize them; you might have run into a few already.

Type 1 - People who say wacky stuff and do strange things; they need unearned love.

Type 2 - People who need you to show up for them; they need unexpected love.

A closer look at both groups will provide valuable perspective on why these groups act as they do and the appropriate, grace-infused response.

For reasons hard to understand, suicide causes some folks to say silly, foolish, or hurtful words. Of course, this happens frequently in everyday interactions too. But after a loved one has taken her own life, a strong desire sets in to hear something that makes sense in a time of despair, so our sensitivity to words increases. Unfortunately, you and the people around you occupy the same space of chaos and confusion that suicide brings and, as one friend describes it well, "fail to engage the brain/mouth barrier." Prepare for empty, shallow, and even strange statements. Prepare for insensitive questions. Prepare for inappropriate, unsolicited advice. Sometimes, all will happen in the same five-minute interaction.

Get ready; such conversations will happen. Repeatedly. Before you launch into the I'll-set-you-straight response that will immediately come to mind, take a deep breath and consider the truth mentioned earlier: Suicide makes no sense to you or the person you've encountered. He or she is verbally processing out of a lack of knowing what to do or say – to help you. The person likely would love to join you on the wailing floor but doesn't know how.

Within a single day of receiving the call about Teri, Becky and I spoke with:

People who tried to relate but really couldn't because they have never had to deal with suicide.

> *She's in a better place now.*
>
> *I can't imagine anyone being that desperate.*
>
> *How horrible.*
>
> *Do you know why she did it?*

People who over-talked in order to relieve their discomfort with how this was wrecking Becky and me.

> *My friend had to deal with someone's suicide and never really go over it.*
>
> *I had a cousin who did the same thing; did I ever tell you what happened with him?*
>
> *I think we should study all the data about how to recognize the warning signs so that this doesn't happen again.*

People who still hurt from someone else's suicide, so their words felt like angry venting.

> *Aren't you mad at her for doing this?*
>
> *This was so cowardly and unfair; make sure you call it "suicide" in your message and don't sugarcoat it.*
>
> *I'll never forgive my brother for his suicide.*

Fortunately, we also encountered a couple sensitive souls willing to hold a long hug, unashamedly shed a tear, and not say much at all. (Keep this approach in mind; it's the best option in many circumstances.)

Grace will radiate from you just from remembering that every person who talks to you, regardless of what they say, feels a desire to come closer to you and to somehow help. No matter whether that happens or not, fixate on the motive and you will dispense grace in abundance – grace that will surprise even you. Especially when you say nothing in those very moments when screaming a response seems so justified. Or would at least momentarily feel good. Enough words will be said in the world today; let the hugs and the tears have their turns. Such is the way of unearned love.

Similar to the volume of words spoken today, plenty of loneliness exists too, so determine now to share grace by showing up for people. Even when you don't have to or want to. Now is likely one of those times. I know the feeling.

Becky and I drove to Indianapolis on a Monday for Teri's funeral scheduled for late Wednesday. We arrived in town early for three reasons: 1) So I could visit the church where the service would take place and discuss logistics with the pastor, 2) To spend time with Teri's family, and 3) To spend time with a group of college friends who knew Teri well.

I looked forward to the church and pastor visit, which would help me feel better prepared to deliver the message at the funeral service. However, I viewed the family and college friends visits as "the right things to do." When faced with uncomfortable situations, apathy often blends well with my internal desire to crawl into a shell and avoid life. Fortunately, lethargy did not win. Time with both groups proved priceless.

Several hours with Teri's parents and sister involved sharing story after story. Laughter and tears alternated frequently throughout our evening; those two responses often travel together, so welcome them both.

A similar time took place 24 hours later with a dozen fellow Purdue University grads who knew and loved Teri. Both nights ended with hugs held long, tears, and reassurances of love.

In those precious moments, and in ways that now make sense, we spent "time on the floor" together.

A suicide typically results in broad collateral damage, leaving holes in countless hearts. While many people will try to ignore, cover, or deny that such a hole exists, one remedy provides the desperately needed backfill. Showing up, in person and when unexpected, strengthens hurting hearts. In the person being visited. And in the person making the visit.

To show up for another person delivers a message of love that words alone can never hope to accomplish. To show up provides a definitive answer to the question "Does anyone care about me?" When you show up, you introduce hope into a time of despair. The unexpected love delivered by physical presence defeats loneliness.

Must you arrive with a forced smile and fake optimism? No. Just as you need not worry about saying the right thing, the profound thing, or anything at all. Just show up – on the floor, in the living room, at the restaurant – to share a hug, a tear, and prolonged quiet moments that would be ruined by words. In companioned stillness a person's soul can honestly feel again; what a gift! Our world needs more silence.

A tangible win for unexpected love took place during Teri's funeral service. Everyone remembered her as fun to be around. But more importantly she was good to be around. She also vivaciously made wonderful stuff happen, often at unexpected times.

We experienced one more such moment in the middle of her funeral when everyone stood, hugged one another, and said "I love you."

We gave grace to one another. Hearts received permission to start healing. And a large gathering of people learned how it feels to give and receive love with little prompting and without any big reason. Who does your heart suggest for a visit, or at least a phone call? Give it a try because you might just change the world, one person's world at a time.

Quite likely, such effort will change two people. Here's what giving grace to others will do to you: Every time you give someone else unearned and unexpected love, especially in a season known more for darkness and despair, you will live into the highest purpose life gives.

"A friend loves at all times."
Proverbs 17:17 (NIV)

Four Corners of Grace

Give-God-Grace Corner

-Comfort-

THIS corner's topic might come as a surprise. Death in any manner creates interest about God, and for good reason; it's the inevitable intersection of life and eternity that everyone will cross. Someone else's journey creates questions about what, where, and who we will find upon passing to the other side. Although some people wonder about the Almighty's existence, no one can argue with this reality: Life is finite; death lasts forever.

Eternity took someone I loved in a manner hard to understand and impossible to accept, so a pressing question emerges: What role does God play in a suicide? This is a fair question to ask, and spending time in the Give-God-Grace Corner will point us toward answers.

A common question many people wonder about when someone takes his own life is whether or not this disqualifies him from entering heaven? Different religious belief systems offer varied answers. And of those answers, the response that made most sense to me also provided the firmest footing I could find. In short, a person's eternity is not determined by his last act on earth.

What a relief, especially when that last act defied logic and reason – and will forever remain that way. Hold on, though; more confusion now enters this corner.

On many occasions, Teri openly talked about being a Christian. Anyone who knew her saw a faith in action, not just in words; the external signs of her faith shone brightly through all the good things she did. Motivated by her beliefs, she financially supported my son in his ministry role. Out of compassion for others, she sent a young Haitian man to college so he could, in turn, help more of his fellow Haitians go to school – even though she had never even met this man. Driven by passion to make a difference, she helped many young people she knew attend private schools and universities in the United States – confident such assistance would help them succeed. She mentored kids, loved people, and served her own family well.

She did it all, in part or in whole, as a Christian motivated by her love for God.

That last sentence might cause a big problem for some and overall confusion for many. Because if she did love God, where was He on January 31 as her last moments unfolded?

The Give-God-Grace-Corner serves as a safe space to ask very real, very heartfelt questions. Some feel they have clear answers found in the Bible; some don't. Sometimes, a sense of relief comes from simply asking.

> *Was God aware of Teri's anxieties and stresses and anything else inside her that contributed to her fateful decision?* Yes, He was.
> "People look at the outward appearance, but the Lord looks at the heart." 1 Samuel 16:7b (NIV)
>
> *Did God see what was going on?* Yes, He did.
> "I am with you and will watch over you wherever you go..." Genesis 28:15 (NIV)

Why didn't God stop her? I don't know. Nobody knows.

Even Billy Graham said he wasn't sure why God lets evil take place. An honest discussion about God and suicide must include sincere confusion caused by verses that seem to promise something quite different, such as:

"The Lord will keep you from all harm – he will watch over your life; the Lord will watch over your coming and going both now and forevermore." Psalm 121:7-8 (NIV)

Yet, the Bible also speaks about the realities of life that we face.

"In this world you will have trouble." John 16:33 (NIV)

We also find confirmation that we will not fully understand the mysteries that surround how life and God work.

"For my thoughts are not your thoughts, neither are your ways my ways," declares the Lord. Isaiah 55:8 (NIV)

Did God truly love her? Yes, He did. Yes, He still does. And yes, He will forever.

How can I be so sure? Unless belief exists that the Bible is filled with lies, comfort shows up in this book in very direct language accessible to anyone. The apostle Paul addresses the issue of God's love in the eighth chapter of Romans:

"I am convinced that nothing can ever separate us from God's love. Neither death nor life, neither angels nor demons, neither our fears for today nor our worries about tomorrow – not even the powers of hell can separate us from God's love." Romans 8:38-39 (NLT)

A close look at this passage reveals an applicability too obvious to quickly skip past:

"Neither death nor life ..." This includes suicide.

"... neither our fears for today nor our worries about tomorrow ..." Teri battled depression.

"... not even the powers of hell ..." Such as the mysterious dark cloud mentioned in the Give-Yourself-Grace chapter.

God, where are You in all this? The answer must come directly from God – not a book, a sermon, or a list of Bible verses.

Please give Him enough grace, enough space, to speak for Himself. Visit the Give-God-Grace corner as many times as you want to ask Him this question and to wrestle with Him about your feelings. He welcomes you in this corner because He wants you to know Him more.

Go there. Find a quiet place. Speak words. Or maybe write them down. He welcomes your pain, your anger, your confusion – because that is where you are right now. So be honest. Be brutally honest with God. Take as much time as you need to express yourself. Then pause and allow quiet to happen, uninterrupted. For a lengthy moment; longer if needed. He waits to meet you; nothing goofy or strange will happen.

Yet maybe articulating the hole in your heart will help it not hurt so much. Maybe in this space a deep breath can take place. Maybe you'll find you're not alone in this corner.

"Draw near to Him and He will draw near to you," the Bible says. Every time I visit this corner, an all-knowing, mysterious, loving God – who wrapped His arms around Teri and tenderly wiped away her tears on January 31 – wipes away my tears too.

The Lord cares deeply when his loved ones die.
Psalm 116:15 (NLT)

Four Corners of Grace

Four Corners of Grace

Give-Teri-Grace Corner

-Freedom-

SUICIDE has claimed a life and now wants to steal as much more life as possible. Including from you. Data shows that those of us left to deal with a loved one's suicide can become high risks themselves – to take their own lives … or at least to never recover.

Failing to recover means I stay bitter. Toward Teri. Toward suicide. Toward God. Toward life. The list could go on.

Why should suicide enjoy such a domino effect?

This question does not imply I must accept suicide and not loathe its reality – just as it doesn't minimize or eliminate my need to grieve. It does, though, suggest that choices exist, starting with how I react to the harsh reality of something I cannot control, in a circumstance I cannot ignore or pretend didn't happen.

Yes, I must accept that a friend is gone and that she departed by ending her own life – a terrible choice she made that means I can no longer enjoy her love and friendship. The finality of that realization makes my hands tremble and eyes water. Many unwanted things in this world are painful to accept, despite a desperate desire that they might not be so.

I can, though, choose to not condemn her – to give Teri grace. Not an excuse or a pardon for what she did. But will anger or resentment change anything, other than my ability to enjoy life? As mentioned before, options exist. I can decide that a healthy mind would never knowingly give up its desire to live. I can decide to extend undeserved merit to the friend now found only in my memory, which will free me from fixating on how her story ended – a pathway that allows me to continue finding and experiencing new joys. Or at least to live better than I would in an existence shackled by bitterness.

These decisions, though, will only happen by visiting the Give-Teri-Grace corner. (Feel free to insert the name of your loved one instead of "Teri.") We travel to this corner last because the grace found here might take quite a while to develop and embrace. That's okay; stay as long as needed – days, weeks, even months. And repeat visits are encouraged.

In the Bible, 13th chapter of the book of John, we read about Jesus at the last supper ... tense room ... tense space with all the people He considered His family. And Jesus said these words:

> "So now I am giving you a new commandment: Love each other. Just as I have loved you, you should love each other. Your love for one another will prove to the world that you are my disciples." John 13:34-35 (NLT)

Wait, this is the Give-Teri-Grace corner. What does love have to do with it?

Plenty.

Over three decades ago, Becky and I abruptly ended our dating relationship. A few months later, Teri approached me at a party, sternly told me to get my [act] together, and to ask Becky to marry me.

While I hoped that Becky had told her to talk to me, Teri had an even higher motivation: "I love my friend, she's family, and I want her to be happy."

On the day Becky and I married, Teri took credit. "Staal, you owe me big time!" she whispered in my ear immediately following the ceremony. And after she gave me a quick peck on the cheek and a big I-told-you-so grin, she turned and joined the celebration. She so loved Becky and me.

I remember that moment every time the urge builds to feel mad at her. Many times, the anger quickly yields to love's strong presence. Of course, resentment too frequently returns without much provocation and sometimes with no warning whatsoever. Just that single memory, though, means I need not feel helpless; I can do something. I can remember that grin. And remember it I must, over and over.

By doing so, I give Teri grace by letting go of her last moments and, instead, embracing the lasting memory of how she loved us. Suicide is denied the opportunity to torment me, and in striking contrast, I keep hold of something much better – oh, how she loved us.

You can do the same. Select that one moment that simultaneously makes you smile and cry because it is such a special memory of the person you miss with all your heart. Keep that memory and recall it often. Write it, talk about it, draw or paint a picture; do whatever you must to keep it always accessible. Then you can rely on it over and over to deliver the grace your heart so powerfully wants to give but doesn't know how. Now you know how.

Several months following the funeral, my wife and I discussed plans for a college group gathering to remember Teri by her graveside. Becky decided she would ask each person to share a single word that represented a memory, one of Teri's many character traits, or any other special meaning. I asked the obvious question, "What word will you share?"

"Forever," Becky said.

"She was my best friend my whole life, and I will live the rest of my days with the memory of her and her love. She will forever remain in my heart."

Other words that members of this group shared included:

Fearless

Vivacious

Joy

Laughter

Inclusive

Welcoming

Bubbly

Cheers!

From "Fearless" to "Forever," each person left this sacred time together with a vocabulary that will trigger memories to honor Teri and ensure that "suicide" is not the final word with which they remember their dear friend. The descriptors they decided upon act as slender slices of Teri's life that they chose to keep tucked in their hearts, capable of prompting healthy tears and honest smiles.

What word will you choose for your loved one? What moment will your heart decide to remember?

Look past cause of death and you will see how a life that leaves behind pieces of love for others to hold onto is a life worth celebrating. Love has a unique ability to shine light into the darkest days, to interrupt tears with a smile, and to heal a broken heart. You will give love the freedom to create something unexpected and amazing when you choose to give grace.

Three things will last forever—faith, hope, and love—and the greatest of these is love.
1 Corinthians 13:13 (NLT)

Four Corners of Grace

Four Corners of Grace

In Closing

-Change-

OUR journey together began with the acknowledgement that hope needs reasons. Stay realistic; start small. Right now, acts that might seem insignificant can serve as markers to let you know you're on the right path. When you wipe tears, surrender to a memory-induced smile, and then take a deep breath in and out, you're taking healthy steps.

Let's be honest, though. The reality of what happened will continue to demand attention. Predictable moments await, such as interacting with friends and family, reunions, a birthday or special anniversary.

Unanticipated moments will also happen, when the pain sneaks up and grabs hold of you by surprise. A song plays. A memory image appears on Facebook. An unexpected entry appears as you scroll through your contact list. Or maybe you talk to someone by the same name. (I sent a happy birthday text to a former co-worker, and emotions engaged as I typed "Happy birthday Teri.") Will this end? Probably never completely. Such is memory's permanent nature. So I give myself grace in new ways as time travels forward; I wipe tears, let a memory conjure a smile, and breathe in and out.

At the start of this book, you and I together set a goal for deep breaths to not hurt so much, I hope you've accomplished that and more by seeing that with grace, breathing does become less painful. Why? I'm not fully certain. But could it be that grace serves as an act of goodness, and even small doses of goodness make a big difference? When you consider grace an option – for yourself, others, God, or the person you lost – a new perspective will emerge.

One that gladly lives beside the pain, does not deny pain's existence, and certainly won't require you to pretend the hurt you feel is anything less than real and okay.

The four corners of grace we visited want you to know they're open for you; they will not force themselves upon you. Grace doesn't work that way. It's available but not mandatory. It's a choice, an option, and sometimes it feels good to know options exist. Especially in defiance of the fear: "Is this the way life will always feel?"

Fortunately, grace carries no requirement for a happy face. You have full permission to reflect whatever is going on inside you right now. Grace will walk with you no matter the condition of your heart and emotions. I wept countless times while typing these pages. You likely did the same while reading.

Maybe giving yourself a little grace gives the lungs a bit more ability to keep breathing when the tears start. Maybe grace toward others will help you feel the warmth found in a hug. Maybe sharing grace in God's direction keeps a door open for exploring more about Him someday. And maybe grace toward the person you lost will, in a special way, keep a relationship going that you would never willingly choose to end. The four corners of grace offer fresh possibilities at a time when change is needed most.

So let those tears fall; wipe them gently. Bring that memory to mind; then savor it. Take in a deep breath; now let it out.

You're going to make it.

And the one sitting on the throne said,
"Look, I am making everything new!"
Revelation 21:5 (NLT)

Four Corners of Grace

Four Corners of Grace

Watch the original Four Corners of Grace message: https://www.davidstaal.net/four-corners-videos.html

To battle America's loneliness epidemic, a key ingredient in too many suicides: https://www.davidstaal.net/the-show-up-book.html

davidstaal.net

Made in the USA
Monee, IL
22 October 2024